The Boys' Book 2

Book 2

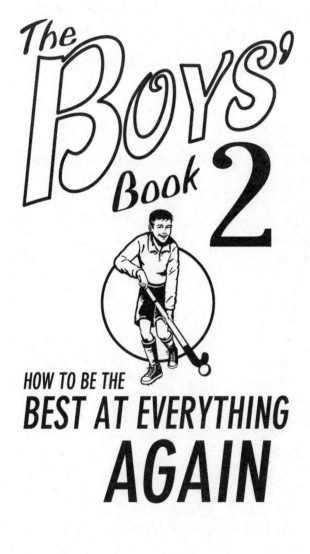

HOW TO BE THE
BEST AT EVERYTHING
AGAIN

Written by Martin Oliver
Illustrated by David Shephard
Edited by Hannah Cohen
Designed by Zoe Quayle

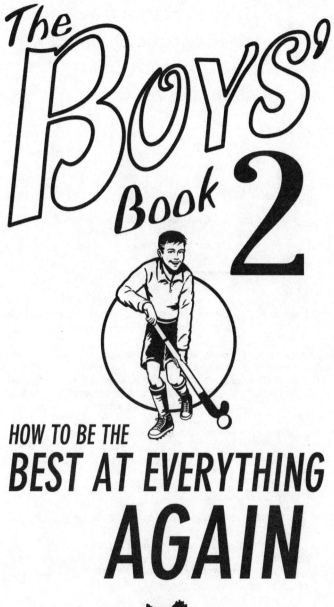

The Boys' Book 2

HOW TO BE THE BEST AT EVERYTHING AGAIN

Buster Books

First published in Great Britain in 2008 by Buster Books,
an imprint of Michael O'Mara Books Limited,
9 Lion Yard, Tremadoc Road, London SW4 7NQ

www.mombooks.com/busterbooks

Text and illustrations copyright © Buster Books 2008
Cover design by Angie Allison (from an original design by www.blacksheep-uk.com)
Cover illustration by Paul Moran

A CIP catalogue record for this book is available from the British Library.

ISBN: 978-1-906082-33-8

4 6 8 10 9 7 5 3

Printed and bound in England by Clays Ltd, St Ives plc

Papers used by Buster Books are natural, recyclable products
made from wood grown in sustainable forests. The manufacturing processes
conform to the environmental regulations of the country of origin.

NOTE TO READERS

CONTENTS

HOW TO PLAY AIR GUITAR

You've got the looks of a rock god and you've got matching attitude to boot. Unfortunately, you haven't quite saved up enough for a stadium-thumping Fender Stratocaster. Don't worry, air guitar is the one instrument everyone can afford and anyone can play, and here's how.

MASTERING THE BASICS

1. Grab your air guitar. Put the strap around your neck and adjust so it is at the right height for you to play comfortably. Strike some poses in front of a mirror to decide whether you want the guitar to sit high up, level with your hips, or lower down, level with your thighs.

2. Practise strumming. This is the key action for any air guitarist. If you're right-handed, strumming is done by moving your right hand up and down over the 'strings', with your palm facing in towards your body. For a variation, you can pretend that you're holding a 'plectrum' – a small triangle-shaped tool used for plucking the strings individually or strumming.

3. Next practise your chord-playing. Chord-playing is when you play several notes at once. To do this press down two or more fingers of your left hand firmly against the 'neck' of your air guitar. Move your hand down the neck for high chords and up the neck for lower chords.

4. Select your music. Find a track with long guitar solos so you can really show off your skills. Listen to the track over and over again until you know it by heart. Practise strumming in time to the music, moving your hands up and down the neck to play the high and low bits of the track.

5. Start to move your whole body – head, legs, hips, shoulders – really get into it.

ADVANCED AIR GUITAR

As you get more confident, start adopting some more extreme poses. Don't be shy. Remember, the more energetic you are when playing the better. Think about jumps, splits, playing the guitar over your head or behind your back. You could even consider smashing the guitar at the end of your performance.

ROCK GOD

A costume will boost your performance. Watch your rock heroes on TV or on the web and copy what they're wearing. Add ripped jeans, a bandana (simply tie a handkerchief around your forehead), pop on some shades and you'll be a true air guitar rock legend.

HOW TO CELEBRATE SCORING A GOAL

How do you make scoring a goal seriously memorable? Easy – just add a special goal celebration afterwards.

The secret to creating a spectacular celebration is to be really imaginative and plan it as much as you can in advance.

WHAT YOU DO

Here's a celebration that is easy to carry off.

1. Before the big match, buy or borrow a fabric pen.

2. Dig out an old white T-shirt or vest. Write a short message on the vest. Go for something such as 'Hello Mum' or 'Beckham Junior', or how about 'Pick me next week, Coach'?

3. Once the writing is dry, pack your T-shirt in with the rest of your kit and take it to the game.

4. When no one in the changing room is looking, pop your T-shirt on under your football shirt.

5. Now go out and play your socks off. As soon as you score, start running towards the corner flag or towards anyone in the crowd you particularly want to impress. Untuck your football shirt and pull it over your head so your T-shirt's message can be clearly seen. Spread your arms and keep running until your teammates catch up with you and congratulate you.

Top Tips. Don't crash into the barriers beside the pitch – this is not cool. Don't celebrate an own goal – you won't be popular!

LOOKING FOR MORE IDEAS?

• **Develop A Trademark Celebration.** Work out a really unique celebration that everyone will associate with you and you alone. Some players celebrate a goal by 'windmilling' one arm or putting both arms out like an aeroplane. One Brazilian superstar was so pleased to become a dad that he rocked his arms like a cradle when he scored. Another player dropped his shorts to reveal Superman pants. Some players celebrate with back flips and somersaults.

• **Player's Props.** Don't be shy about using props. Players have celebrated goals by putting on masks, or sucking a baby's dummy. The sky's the limit – so long as you can carry the props on to the pitch without being stopped by the referee.

HOW TO PITCH A TENT

Nothing beats the feeling of crawling out of the rain into your tent after a hard day of trekking in the great outdoors. Here are some top tips to prepare you for pitching your tent like a pro.

THE PERFECT PLACE TO PITCH

- Look for a spot to put up your tent well before it gets dark. If you're not staying on an official site, ask permission before pitching your tent.

- Choose a site that is not in a valley or a ditch. If you choose either of those places and it rains, your tent could flood.

- Choose a spot that is sheltered from the wind. If you pitch your tent on an exposed area or on the top of a hill you and your tent may risk being blown away!

- Choose somewhere as flat as possible. If there is a slight slope, it's best to make sure you sleep with your head higher than your feet.

- Check for any signs of animal tracks or insects. Camping on an ants' nest could result in a serious case of 'ants in your pants'.

PITCHING THE TENT

Each tent is different – some tents will pop up by themselves, some require poles and flysheets. Therefore, it is essential that you practise pitching your tent in a garden or park before an expedition. Get familiar with how your tent works, so you can put it up quickly when night is falling and time is short.

Never leave home without checking all the pieces of your tent are in the bag and the instructions are packed.

When pegging out the groundsheet of your tent, make sure it is stretched out as flat as possible. Use a rubber mallet to bash the metal pegs through the loops. If you have a separate groundsheet, always make sure that the groundsheet is tucked up inside the tent to ensure no water can get in.

When your tent is up, peg down the guy ropes so your tent is standing up without any creases. (Guy ropes are the ropes on the outside of the tent.) When you're putting the pegs into the ground, put them in at an angle of 45°, leaning away from the tent. The ropes should pull on them at an angle of 90°.

If it looks like rain, slacken the guy ropes slightly. This will reduce the chance of the pegs being dragged out of the ground or the tent material tearing in a heavy shower.

STRIKING YOUR TENT

When it's time to take your tent down – known as 'striking' your tent – always take up the groundsheet first. Turn it upside down to allow it to dry and brush off any grass or mud.

Pull the pegs out of the ground one by one. If you struggle to pull your tent pegs out, tap them backwards and forwards with the mallet to loosen them.

Try and dry your tent before packing it away. If you have to pack it up wet, dry it as soon as possible or it may rot.

Warning. Before you leave to go camping, make sure you tell an adult where you are going. Always carry a mobile phone on an expedition so you can let an adult know where you are at all times.

HOW TO MAKE A TANGRAM

Tangrams are a type of puzzle invented long ago in ancient China.

You will need to cut up a square of stiff card into seven sections as shown here.

The object of a tangram puzzle is to rearrange the seven pieces of a square into different shapes to form a recognisable image. It is incredible how many shapes you can make using just the seven pieces of card.

To start you off, here are some shapes that you can make by rearranging the pieces you have cut out. When you've done these, see how many more shapes you can make.

A rabbit sunbathing

A person cleaning a car

Relaxing in the garden

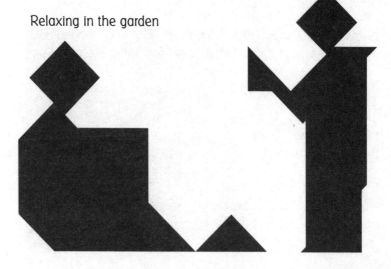

HOW TO BOIL AN EGG

If you want to be sure you never starve learn how to rustle up a delicious soft-boiled egg. You could even earn some extra pocket money by making your parents a boiled egg with toast for breakfast in bed.

BE PREPARED

Take your eggs out of the fridge about 20 minutes before you boil them. If you take eggs straight from the fridge and put them into boiling water, they are quite likely to crack.

If you forget to take your eggs out of the fridge in time and you are in a hurry, run them under a warm tap for a minute.

Don't choose really fresh eggs to boil – you will find that their shells are hard to peel off once they are boiled. Instead choose eggs that are roughly five days old.

Find a saucepan just large enough for the eggs you want to boil. If you use a pan that is too large, your eggs may move around and crack against each other or on the side of the pan.

WHAT YOU DO

1. Pour some cold water in the saucepan. Bring the water to the boil.

2. Put a small pinprick in each of the eggs. This allows any steam to exit and will prevent cracking.

3. Place each egg on a spoon and gently lower into the saucepan.

4. Reduce the heat so the water is no longer boiling but 'simmering' (bubbling gently).

5. Set your timer. The length of time you cook each egg depends on how you (or your folks) like their eggs.

Timing. If you are using large or medium-sized eggs, cook your eggs for exactly three minutes – this will give you a perfectly-cooked egg with a deliciously runny yolk. If you are boiling extra-large eggs, five minutes' cooking will leave the yolk runny. Seven minutes will mean it is only very slightly runny.

6. Once the cooking time is up, carefully pick up each egg with the spoon and pop them in eggcups, with the rounder end of the egg at the bottom.

HOW TO SURVIVE AT SEA

You're cruising at a rate of knots, riding the crest of a wave, when suddenly your boat begins to sink. The gently-lapping sea instantly becomes a treacherous ocean. In order to survive you are going to need skill, endurance, luck – and the following tips.

STAY ON BOARD

You're more likely to survive at sea on a boat than on a life raft, so don't rush to abandon ship. Even if your boat is damaged, you're almost certainly better off on board. Why? Because the bigger the boat, the more visible it will be to a rescue party, and the better protected you are from the wind, water and sun.

PROPER PROVISIONS

If you have to leave your boat because it sinks, then your life raft should be equipped with a basic survival kit. This will include a short-wave radio, a GPS receiver (a Global Positioning System receiver which can calculate your exact position in the ocean), a compass, a knife, self-igniting flares, a waterproof watch, a waterproof torch, warm blankets, a box of matches in a waterproof container, a first-aid kit and some dry food. However, the most important thing you should have on board is fresh water. A lack of fresh, clean water will dramatically reduce the number of days you can stay alive.

Warning. No matter how thirsty you get, NEVER be tempted to drink seawater. Seawater is three times as salty as your blood and your body would not be able to cope. It would also make you extremely thirsty.

You will also need to eat. There should be provisions in your raft, but once these are used up, don't panic. Fish should be plentiful in the ocean and flying fish may even land in your raft. If you don't have a fishing rod then try using twine and hooks made from wire or aluminium cans.

You can eat the flesh of fish raw. Don't forget to eat the eyes as well. Gross, but these contain water, too. Make sure you don't eat the organs or you may become sick.

STAY DRY

Seawater is your number one enemy, so your main aim should be to keep dry and stay warm. If you are out in cold weather, you could develop 'hypothermia' (a condition that sets in when your body temperature drops below its normal level). This can kill within a very short space of time. If you're adrift in hot weather, exposure to seawater and sun can damage your skin, leading to blisters and other infections.

So if your life raft has a canopy, use it. If not, try to rig up sheets and blankets as a shelter from the waves and from the sun as soon as possible. If you remain exposed, you will survive for a shorter time than if you are under cover.

STAY OR GO?

Even if you know your location, attempting to row towards land may not be your best strategy. Currents and riptides may push you further from your destination and your efforts to row the life raft may waste precious energy.

If your boat was able to send a distress signal before it sank, staying close to where you sent the flare will mean that you are more likely to be found by potential rescuers.

SIGNAL AND SURVIVE

A survivor in a life raft will be almost invisible in the vast seascape. As a result, it's vital you are ready to signal to any passing plane or ship. If you have self-igniting flares and a short-wave radio then make sure you know how to use them so you are ready to swing into action at any time.

If you don't have either device, use a hand-held mirror to reflect sunlight towards rescuers, or attract attention by using a whistle or a torch. As a last resort, waving brightly-coloured material may also be effective.

Warning. Before setting out on a voyage, always tell someone your route and the time you will arrive at your destination. This way people will know where to look if you don't arrive.

HOW TO MAKE A COWPAT FLOAT

Like ice cream? Like cola? Well, there's an easy way to double your enjoyment by making your very own 'cowpat' float.

You Will Need:

• cola • chocolate ice cream • a spoon
• a straw • an ice-cold glass

WHAT YOU DO

1. Pour cold water over the outside of a large glass, then put it straight into the freezer. Leave it for around 15 minutes until the thin layer of water on the outside of the glass freezes.

2. Take the glass out of the freezer and add two scoops of the chocolate ice cream.

3. Pour cola slowly into the glass. It will fizz and rise, so don't rush it. (If the bubbles start to overflow the top of the glass, place your index finger on the rim of the glass to burst them.)

4. Grab your spoon and tuck in. Use your straw to reach the cola at the bottom of the glass.

HOW TO BE A ROCKET SCIENTIST

You can make sure your career as a rocket scientist takes off using a few things you can find around your house.

You Will Need:

- some water • a packet of effervescent, soluble aspirin
- an empty plastic 35 mm film container with a tight-fitting lid (ask for spare ones at a film-developing shop)

WHAT YOU DO

Fill a film canister a quarter full with water (too much water will make your rocket too heavy to lift off – you should experiment to get the right amount).

Head outside because firing rockets is messy.

Pop one of the effervescent tablets in the container and quickly seal the lid tightly. Place the canister on the ground – lid side down.

Stand well back and watch as your rocket launches into the sky.

Warning. Do not stand directly over your rocket once it is made – you will find yourself in the line of fire.

HOW TO PRESERVE A TOOTH

If you or a friend has a tooth knocked out – playing football, rugby or in an accidental collision – don't panic. These simple steps might help you preserve the tooth long enough for it to be popped back in by a dentist. You'll soon be smiling again.

1. Find your tooth! Don't touch the root. Hold it by the 'enamel' – the hard, white, outer coating.

2. Run home. Clean your tooth thoroughly, rinsing it in milk (not tap water) to remove any blood, earth or grime.

3. Find a clean plastic container with a lid and put the tooth in it. Cover the tooth completely with milk.

4. Take the tooth (and yourself) off to your dentist as quickly as you can (within one to three hours of the accident). If you've followed these instructions, you'll have a 50/50 chance of having your tooth successfully refitted.

HOW TO PERFORM A PERFECT ROUND-OFF

A 'round-off' is a more impressive stunt than a cartwheel, but it takes a bit more skill and practice to master. It starts off exactly the same as a cartwheel, but you should bring your feet together while you are upside down and land facing the direction you came from.

Follow the steps below to perfect your round-off. Make sure you practise on a gym mat.

1. Start with your right foot forwards if you are right-handed (left foot forwards if you are left-handed). Extend your arms above your head as shown.

2. Lunge forwards, placing both hands on the mat, one after the other (as if you were going to perform a cartwheel). Kick your legs up, one-by-one, until they end up side-by-side stretched vertically above your head for a moment.

Top Tips. Be prepared to absorb the impact of your landing by bending your knees slightly as your feet hit the mat. If you find yourself offbalance when you land, add a small jump rather than a step, as this will look like part of the move.

3. Twist your body as you snap your legs back down to the mat.

4. When you land on the mat you should be facing the direction from which you came. Your round-off is complete.

HOW TO ESCAPE FROM A BURNING HOUSE

House fires are rare but they can be deadly – so make it your job to check that everyone in your household knows exactly what to do in an emergency. Here are some useful tips.

BE PREPARED

Appoint yourself the fire marshal of your household. Insist that your home has well-positioned smoke alarms fitted around the house (at least one on each floor). Make it your job to check each alarm at least once a week to see that the batteries are working. Never, ever let anyone in your family 'borrow' the batteries from the alarms to use in toys or other appliances.

FIRE!

As soon as you become aware that there is smoke in the house make sure everyone is awake and ready to get out of the building quickly. Do not stop to take anything with you. Your things can be replaced, you can't.

If you can get out through a door, touch it with the back of your hand before opening it. If it is cool, it's probably safe to go through. Turn your face away then open it a crack to make sure.

Smoke and fumes rise, making the air down by the floor clearer and easier to breath, so crawl to an exit on your hands and knees.

Once you're through, shut the door behind you. This can slow the progress of a fire down by as much as ten minutes.

If the door is hot when you touch it, take an alternative route to safety. If you're heading out through a window, make sure you know how to open it. If you need to break the glass, cover it with a sheet, a towel or a pillow. Protect your hand and arm with fabric as well. Smash all the glass out of the frame so you don't cut yourself climbing through the window.

If you are trapped in a room with running water (the bathroom or the kitchen), soak tea towels, curtains, pillowcases or blankets in water and stuff them into any cracks that are under the doors or between the floorboards. This will stop smoke seeping into the room.

Dial the emergency services as soon as possible. Once help arrives, let the professionals do their job – they're trained and equipped to do it. Once you are outside, get as far away from the building as possible and check everyone is out.

HOW TO TIE A CLOVE HITCH

A 'clove hitch' is one of the most useful knots you can learn, allowing you to attach a rope to almost anything. Use a clove hitch to moor a boat, secure a rope when rock climbing, or simply attach a piece of string to a paper clip!

Practise the simple steps below to attach a piece of rope to a rock-climbing clip, known as a 'karabiner'.

1. Make two identical loops with your rope.

2. Slide the loop on the right in front of the loop on the left.

3. Open the karabiner's gate (the clip part) and lift the two loops through the gate.

Pull both ends of your rope down to tighten the clove hitch.

the gate

HOW TO BE GOOD AT NAMING CAPITAL CITIES

Have you noticed that geography tests, TV quizzes and general knowledge questions nearly always ask about capital cities? Impress everyone with your exceptional knowledge by memorising this A to Z list of capital cities.

Australia – Canberra

Belarus – Minsk

Chile – Santiago

Dominican Republic – Santo Domingo

Ethiopia – Addis Ababa

Finland – Helsinki

Ghana – Accra

Haiti – Port-au-Prince

Indonesia – Jakarta

Jamaica – Kingston

Korea (North) – Pyongyang

Korea (South) – Seoul

Lithuania – Vilnius

Mongolia – Ulan Bator

Nepal – Kathmandu

Oman – Muscat

Papua New Guinea – Port Moresby

Qatar – Doha

Rwanda – Kigali

Slovenia – Ljubljana

Tanzania – Dar es Salaam

Uruguay – Montevideo

Vietnam – Hanoi

Wales – Cardiff

Yemen – Sana'a

Zimbabwe – Harare

HOW TO BE A MEMORY MASTER

If you've been getting dates wrong in your history tests, forgetting to record your favourite TV programme, or if your puppy is starving because you forgot to buy his biscuits – don't worry. Here are some ways to turn yourself into a memory master.

PRACTICE MAKES PERFECT

Play this game with your friends to keep your memory in peak condition. Before your friends arrive, collect 20 objects and put them on a table. Here are some suggestions:

- a pencil • a plastic toy • a DVD • a mug • a sock
- a fishing rod • an ice cream cone • a mobile phone
- a stone • a key • a paper clip • a baseball cap • a book
- a spoon • an apple • a sugar cube • scissors
- a ruler • a watch • a yo-yo

Now cover all the objects with a cloth. When your friends are gathered round, lift the cloth for 20 seconds. Then cover the table again and get everyone to write down every object they can remember. The person who remembers the most wins.

MEMORY TECHNIQUES

Here are some tips to help you remember things:

• Ever wondered why you can remember your team's results but not the name of some old king? It is the joy (and misery) that you experience following your team that makes it easier to remember their triumphs (and defeats). Try to attach some emotion to the information that you need to remember by finding out some more interesting details – for example, Prince Albert died of typhoid in 1861. His widow, Queen Victoria, wore black every day until her own death forty years later. By knowing that fact, you will be far more likely to remember the date of his death.

• Try to make memorable mental pictures of things you need to remember. For example, if you keep forgetting to feed a pet, imagine it doing something crazy like nibbling the roof of your house. This visual image will pop into your mind, triggering your memory.

• Rhymes and memorable sentences are great ways to make remembering information easier. Here's a useful way to remember the names of all the planets and their order in the solar system, starting with the nearest to the Sun. (In case you were wondering Pluto is no longer officially a planet.)

My **V**ery **E**ducated **M**other **J**ust **S**erved **U**s **N**oodles.

The first letter of each word in this sentence is the same as the first letter of each of the planets:

Mercury, **V**enus, **E**arth, **M**ars, **J**upiter, **S**aturn, **U**ranus, **N**eptune.

Try making up sentences for things you need to remember.

HOW TO BE A YO-YO STAR

Once you've mastered the basic up and down yo-yo motion, it's time to turn on the star quality as you master a 'Sleeper', throw a 'Forward Pass' and 'Walk The Dog'. You will need a good quality yo-yo and some serious practice to master the moves described below.

THE SLEEPER

The idea of the Sleeper is to gain enough control of your yo-yo that, instead of bouncing back up to you, the yo-yo 'sleeps'.

Hold the yo-yo in your palm with the back of your hand facing downwards. Bend your arm up towards your shoulder and, as you straighten it, smoothly release the yo-yo from your hand, flicking it out and down towards the floor with your wrist.

When the yo-yo reaches its lowest point, keep your hand still for a while. This will ensure the yo-yo 'sleeps' at the end of the string, still spinning but not coming back up. After a few seconds, turn your hand face down and jerk the yo-yo back up.

THE FORWARD PASS

Hold the yo-yo in your palm with the back of your hand facing upwards. Instead of dropping the yo-yo towards the floor, throw it out horizontally in front of you. When it reaches the end of the string, jerk to bring it back. Turn your hand so you catch the yo-yo in the palm of your hand.

WALK THE DOG

Throw a Sleeper (see opposite) towards a flat floor. When the yo-yo is 'sleeping', lower it onto the floor. As soon as the yo-yo makes contact with the floor it will start rolling away from you. Tug the string to bring the yo-yo up to your hand.

HOW TO ESCAPE FROM AN ANGRY BULL

Next time you're out in the countryside, keep your eyes peeled and stay out of fields that contain any large, menacing bull-like shapes – especially if that large, menacing bull-like shape is on its own. Bulls are generally happier when they are close to cows. However, if you do find yourself in the middle of a field with an angry bull, here's what to do.

STAY STILL

Don't approach it, and do everything you can to stop the bull noticing you. Hard as it sounds, you should resist any instinct to run. A bull can smell and hear better than people, but it can't see very well. If you move, that will attract its attention.

Always keep the bull in sight and once it has moved away from you or doesn't seem interested in you any more, start heading slowly and steadily towards the gate of the field.

CHARGE!

If it is too late and the bull is heading your way, it is time to run. Bulls are fast movers and can easily outrun a person. As a result, you need to look for cover in a nearby building or behind a solid gate or fence.

As the bull charges towards you, do your best to try to distract him. Take off your jacket and swing it wildly in the air to attract the bull's attention. Then, before the bull gets too close, throw your jacket as far away from yourself as possible. The bull should go to investigate it rather than you. Repeat with as many layers of clothing as you have until you reach safety.

Top Tip. Don't panic if you find you are wearing something red – bulls don't react to red any more than any other colour.

Warning. Never walk a dog through a field of cattle. All cattle, especially bulls, hate dogs and if they spot one they will be far more likely to get grumpy.

HOW TO UNDO A JAMMED JAR LID

Impress your family and friends with your strength and skill at undoing the most stubborn of jam-jar lids.

HOT WATER

If the lid is made of metal, run hot water over it for about 20 seconds (take care not to scald yourself). Alternatively, fill a basin with hot water and stand the jar in it upside down, so the water covers the lid completely. Never use boiling water as it might cause the glass of the jar to crack.

Dry the lid thoroughly with a towel. Pop on some rubber washing-up gloves (to help you grip) and twist the lid.

OPEN SESAME

If the lid is still stuck, turn the jar upside down and carefully bang the lid firmly on a hard surface. Repeat this two or three times, then twist the lid. It should easily come undone.

Top Tip. All screw-thread lids undo anticlockwise (when viewed from above).

HOW TO BE TOP DOG

Although you can actually teach an old dog new tricks, there's no doubt that it's easier to train and improve the obedience of a puppy. If you are lucky enough to get a puppy this is a great opportunity for you to spend some quality time with the fluffiest member of your family. What's more, by putting in some effort at the start, your puppy will be sure to grow up knowing that you are top dog.

LIE DOWN

1. Get your puppy to sit in front of you while you hold its collar. Have a treat in your hand and show it to the puppy.

2. Lower the treat towards the ground so that your puppy must move its whole body downwards to keep its eyes on the treat. Keep hold of your puppy's collar so it can't gobble it up.

3. Say 'down' clearly, as your puppy begins to move downwards.

4. If you're having trouble, you can encourage your puppy by gently picking up its front legs and lowering it to the ground. Don't forget to restate the command 'down' while you are doing this.

5. Once your puppy is lying on the floor, give it the treat.

6. Keep repeating the exercise but replace the reward with ear-tickling, neck-scratching and generally making a big fuss every time your puppy obeys.

GOOD DOG!

- **Short And Fun.** Keep your pup-training sessions short and fun so your furry friend enjoys each lesson.

- **Keep It Simple.** Give your puppy one, clear instruction to follow – it is just a young animal and will not be able to cope with anything unclear. Repeat every task again and again to make sure it sticks in your puppy's memory.

- **Be Consistent.** Your puppy will be confused if you change your mind. So, if he or she is not allowed upstairs on your bed, make it clear that they must not go on the beds – ever!

- **Good Dog.** Be positive and offer lots of encouragement (and rewards) to your puppy. Don't punish bad behaviour but make it clear that it won't be tolerated. Always reward good behaviour with plenty of cuddles.

HOW TO SURVIVE A TERRIBLE HAIRCUT

If you've ever been on the receiving end of the haircut from hell, turning you from 'too cool for school' into 'too embarrassed for class', read on for some helpful tips on toughing it out.

- **Take A Shower.** Even the worst hair disasters usually look better after a good soak, shampoo and dry. At the very least, it'll stop your neck itching. At the very best, you might be able to salvage something.

- **Get Professional Help.** Go to your local barber or hairdresser to see if they can repair the damage.

- **Take Drastic Action.** Turn your wonky fringe and tufty clumps of hair into a 'crew cut', a short all-over style. Ask your mum first if you are allowed to have a crew cut. Get a pair of clippers and hand them to someone you trust – a crew cut is almost impossible to mess up. You may have cold ears for a while but at least you'll look cool and save a fortune on gel.

- **Get A Hat.** A terrible haircut is the perfect excuse to get your parents to stump up for that cool baseball cap you've been asking for. Of course, you'll have to take it off at some point but then you can blame your new look on hat-hair!

HOW TO RIDE A CAMEL

Camels may not be a common sight in places such as Western Europe and the USA, but in other parts of the world they have been used for hundreds of years to carry goods and people.

Camels' long strides and strong backs make riding them fast and fun. They can reach speeds of up to 60 kilometres per hour. Camel-racing is hugely popular in Australia and the Middle East.

If you're ever given the chance to hop on board one of these one- or two-humped creatures, here's what you should know.

FIND A SUITABLE CAMEL

Don't even think about trying to ride an untrained camel unless you're prepared to visit a hospital. Find a domesticated camel, with a trained handler.

Make sure the camel has already been raked to remove any grit, stones or burrs that would scratch if you mounted it. If not, rake the camel with a garden rake.

The saddle is secured with straps so that it is flexible enough to move with the camel's motion without slipping off altogether. Ask the handler to check that the saddle has been fastened securely and will not fall off when you hop aboard.

GETTING ON BOARD

Unless you have a raised platform, the camel will have to kneel or lie down for you to clamber on. Ask the handler to rest one foot on the camel's front leg to make sure that the camel does not get up before you are ready.

Put one foot in one of the stirrups then throw your other leg over the saddle. Try to do this with confidence to show your camel you mean business.

Settle yourself in the saddle and be prepared for the camel to stand up. Lean back, as the camel will bring its back legs up first. Then lean forwards as its front legs come up.

STEERING YOUR CAMEL

Like horses, camel-riders use reins to direct their mounts. Unlike horses, however, the reins are usually attached to a peg inside the camel's nose. Hold the reins confidently without tugging or pulling them. Pulling them too hard will be painful and annoy your camel – and you don't want to be riding a cross camel.

To turn right, apply slight pressure on the rein in your right hand. Do the opposite to turn left. Relax the reins when your camel is heading in the right direction, because it will become confused if you maintain constant pressure.

Ask the handler to attach a leading rein to your camel – this can be used to lead and guide your camel while you are learning.

GETTING IN THE SWING

Riding a walking camel is surprisingly comfortable. Unlike horses, a camel sways from side to side because it lifts both feet on the same side at the same time when walking forwards. Always move with the sway of the camel – if you fight the sway you will have a hard time staying in the saddle.

Top Tip. Your camel will respond better if you aren't nervous and jittery, so relax and enjoy the ride.

DISMOUNTING

When you are done, you will need to get your camel to kneel down again so you can dismount. Ask the handler to pull down gently on the leading rein and, at the same time, tap lightly on the camel's front legs with a stick. As the handler does this, you must give the command 'koosh!' which is 'lie down!' in camel language. Your camel should obediently drop to his knees.

Once the camel is kneeling or lying ready for you to get off, stand up in the stirrups and throw one leg back over the hump. Jump or step down.

Make sure you pat the camel to show you appreciate its patience.

HOW TO BE A MASTER OF DISGUISE

Disguising yourself is a useful skill if you want to throw someone off your tracks or follow someone you know without being recognised.

A good disguise will simply allow you to move around unnoticed. To do this, it's a good idea not to draw attention to yourself. The less noticeable you are, the less time people will spend looking at you and the more successful your disguise is likely to be.

BE PREPARED

Think carefully about what you need to create your disguise and whether it will all fit in your rucksack or school bag. You never know when you might need it.

Here are a few ideas for your portable disguise kit:

- reversible jacket or top • hat • glasses or sunglasses
- comb • styling gel • baggy clothes • cotton-wool balls
- stick-on tattoos • fake nose • a wig (make sure your wig is a different style or colour to your real hair – your local fancy-dress shop should be able to supply you with one)

CHANGE YOUR BODY SHAPE

If you're a bit on the skinny side, try to make yourself seem fatter. Wear extra layers of clothing – this will also change the way you move. Stuffing balls of cotton wool in your cheeks will completely change the shape of your face. Take care not to swallow them, you might choke!

If you're not very tall, try to make yourself seem taller. Wear shoes with heels rather than flat shoes, spike up your hair and don't slouch. Alternatively, you could always try hunching your shoulders to change how you look from behind.

CHANGE YOUR WALK

If possible, ask a friend to video you walking. This is a great way to see what other people see. Analyse your movements and think hard about how you could change them.

If you usually bounce along full of energy, try to slow yourself down. Walk more slowly and make your movements heavy and more clumsy.

If you walk slowly already, practise walking faster. Try walking on the balls of your feet or leaning forwards. Ask your friend to video your new walk and see if you can see the difference. You could try taking bigger steps when you walk, or even adopting a slight limp.

CHANGE YOUR TALK

The way you talk and interact with other people is often a real give away. Try to change small things about your voice, by speaking more slowly or at a lower pitch. Talking in a higher pitch might just make you laugh!

CONFIDENCE IS KEY

The most important thing, however you disguise yourself, is to act natural and confident. Nothing will give you away faster than if you are hesitant or awkward in your new disguise – this will quickly arouse suspicion.

HOW TO TALK LIKE A SURFER

Much more important than wearing the right gear is knowing how to talk like a chilled-out surfer dude. If you don't want to be seen as a monstrous 'poseur', it's time to get pumped about surfer speak!

Stoked – Elated	**Shred** – To go well or go fast
Blast Some Air – Jump (on a board)	**Chill** – To relax
Killer – Superb	**Rents** – Parents
Poseur – Someone trying to be a surfer dude	**Grommet** – Beginner surfer
Odious Maximus – Arousing hatred	**Barney / Kook** – A bad surfer
Bogus – Inferior	**Scarfage** – Food
Heinous – Terrible, awful	**Yo** – Hello
Space – To forget	**Howzit?** – How's it going?
Grizzle – To sleep well	**Later** – Bye
	Hasta – Bye

HOW TO TIE A BOW TIE LIKE JAMES BOND

One of the most amazing things about James Bond – after the stunts, the gadgets and cars – is his ability to look cool when he's wearing a bow tie. If you've ever tried to put one on yourself, you'll know it's easier to wrestle with all sorts of wild animals than tie your own bow tie – until now. Follow the steps below to achieve bow-tie perfection.

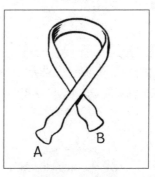

1. Place the tie around your neck, with one end pulled slightly longer (end A) than the other (end B).

2. Now cross end A over end B.

3. Take end A and tuck it under end B and up under your chin, as shown.

4. Take end B and make it into a loop.

5. Hold the loop with one finger while you bring end A over it.

6. Now double end A back on itself, pushing it through the loop at the back of the bow tie.

7. For the final, 'shaken-but-not-stirred' look, adjust both ends and tighten your perfect bow tie.

Mission accomplished.

HOW TO DO SOME DAMAGE WITH THE FINGER OF DOOM

Gather your friends and tell them that you possess a fearsome finger of destruction – a digit so dangerous, you can dent cans with it. All you need is an empty tin can (the kind that beans or tomatoes come in), some friends, a bit of practice and some acting skills.

1. Bring out your tin can and challenge your friends to dent or crush the tin in any way using only one finger (no throwing or stamping allowed). The tin will remain undamaged.

2. Take the tin and lie it on its side on the ground. Inform your audience you will dent it using one finger alone.

3. Put the index finger of your strongest hand across the middle of the tin. Then smack the finger with the palm of your other hand. The tin will dent and you can take a bow.

HOW TO MAKE
A MAGIC CUP OF COFFEE

Here's how to perform a trick that will convince your audience you have a bottomless cup of coffee.

You Will Need:

- a full cup of coffee and a saucer • two sugar cubes
- a gullible friend

WHAT YOU DO

1. Hold the cup and saucer in your left hand. Hold one sugar cube clearly in your right hand and conceal the other cube under the saucer in your left hand.

2. Tip the cup and saucer very slightly towards your audience. This will ensure that the hidden sugar cube is completely concealed under the saucer.

3. Drop the cube in your right hand into the cup of coffee. The instant the sugar cube hits the bottom of the cup, drop the sugar cube out of your left hand onto the floor.

It's all about timing, so practise until you can make it look as if one sugar cube is falling through a bottomless coffee cup.

HOW TO CRACK A WHIP

If you've ever watched a cowboy movie, or admired Indiana Jones at the cinema, then you'll know how cool cracking a whip can look. Here's how to get in on the whip-cracking act.

FIRST YOU NEED A WHIP

- There are four main types of whip suitable for cracking – bullwhips, signalwhips, snakewhips and stockwhips.

- It is the 'popper' – the frayed end of these types of whips – that makes the cracking noise you want. So choose a whip that has a frayed end and a knot or lashing behind the fraying.

- Whips can be as long as 8 metres, but to get cracking it's a good idea to choose one of the shorter ones – roughly 1.5 metres long. Make sure you get a whip that you can hold comfortably. It should fit into the palm of your hand so you can keep a good grip on it.

- If you can't get hold of a whip, tie about 2 metres of clothes line securely to a piece of bamboo cane. Tie a knot at the loose end of the line, too. This will help you practise the basic whipping movement, but it sadly won't make that desired cracking noise.

WEAR PROTECTIVE GEAR

Learning to crack a whip can be a painful business. Get it wrong and you will whip yourself, so wear a pair of sunglasses to protect your eyes, a denim jacket or shirt and long trousers. Gloves are essential, too.

Warning. Find a space where there are no objects, animals or people within range of your whip. NEVER crack a whip at any person or animal.

Grip the handle of your whip firmly in the palm of your strongest hand. Place the other end on the floor and walk backwards in a straight line so the whip stretches out in front of you. The key is to make sure that the whip is perfectly straight. If it isn't, there is a good chance you will whip your leg as you swing it.

PRACTISE SWINGING

Start with your whip arm relaxed by your side, with your hand pointing towards the floor.

Bending your arm at the elbow, swing your arm up so your hand ends up above your shoulder. The palm of your hand should now be beside your head, facing your ear. Your elbow should be pointing forwards, in the direction you want the whip to travel. You should try and make this a smooth, fluid movement – not jerky.

If you do this swing correctly, the speed at which you swing your arm should be enough to extend the whip fully in the air behind you. Put your arm back down by your side and practise the swing again.

THE CRACKING ACTION

Once you've mastered a smooth swing, it's time to work up to cracking the whip. As you swing up, take a step forwards with the opposite leg to the hand you're using to hold the whip. As your foot lands, and your whip hand reaches its position beside your ear, snap your wrist forwards using the same movement as you would if you were hammering a nail. Your whip will snap forwards, too.

Keep moving your arm forwards until it is straight out in front of you, horizontal to the ground – no lower than this or the whip will hit the ground. This motion should create a loop in the whip and the really cool, loud cracking sound you are looking for.

HOW TO EAT WITCHETTY GRUBS

The witchetty grub is a particularly 'delicious' type of moth larva found in the Australian bush and is sometimes eaten by the Aboriginal people who live there.

Here are two ways to enjoy tucking in to a witchetty grub:

- **Raw.** Lower the wriggling beastie into your mouth. Bite it at the neck and start chewing as quickly as you can.

Raw witchetty grubs taste like nutty-flavoured cream once you bite into them. Delicious.

• **Grub Soup.** Take the heads off your grubs. Fry a handful of grubs in some cooking oil until their skins are crispy. Add some chopped onions, salt and pepper. Pour in a half a litre of chicken stock and cook for half an hour. Cooked witchetty grubs taste like a cross between roast chicken and scrambled eggs.

Top Tip. If you can't get hold of any witchetty grubs, simply replace them with prawns when making your soup. Prepare each prawn by pulling the head and legs off and peeling the skin away. You don't need to tell your friends you have used prawns, though.

Warning. It is a good idea to stick with prawns, as it is essential to know exactly what bug you are eating and that it is safe to eat, and not the larva of a protected species.

HOW TO HYPNOTISE SOMEONE

Hypnosis is widely recognised as a powerful tool that can be used to influence the mind and change the way people think. Read on to find out how you can hypnotise your friends. Imagine being able to get them to do whatever you want ...

TEST YOUR SUBJECTS

You can test which of your friends is going to be easiest to hypnotise. Ask each of them to roll their eyes as far up in their sockets as they can. The further their eyes disappear upwards, the better a candidate they are.

STARTING HYPNOSIS

1. Choose somewhere calm, quiet, safe and without any distractions.

2. A person can only be hypnotised if he is completely relaxed, so begin by telling your friend to lie down and close his eyes. Ask him to take a deep breath and, as he breathes out, to relax his hands, arms, shoulders, neck, head, stomach, legs and feet.

Always talk in a gentle, soothing voice. The more relaxed your friend becomes the more likely he is to succumb to your hypnotic powers. Don't use props such as a watch or swinging pendulum – they are more likely to distract your subject than hypnotise them.

3. Reminding your friend to keep his eyes closed, ask him to do something simple like move the middle finger of his right hand up and down. Repeat this instruction a few times. If he doesn't do it, return to the task of relaxing him.

4. If he does do what you say, you can move on to make some more powerful suggestions. Here are a couple you could try:

- Tell him that a fly is buzzing around his ears and see if he tries to swat it away.

- Suggest that there is a strong smell in the room and check if his nose wrinkles up.

Build up your suggestions slowly and don't make far-fetched requests. Don't jump in and ask him to act like a chicken – there is little chance he will do it and a suggestion that is too silly might wake him up.

FINISHING A SESSION

To bring your friend out of his trance-like state, simply say 'I am now going to count to five. When I reach five, your eyes will open and you will wake up feeling relaxed and refreshed!'

HOW TO FAKE A SCAR

Want to convince your friends you have a terrible scar, or simply need to look the part for a Halloween party? Follow these instructions to make a realistic-looking, gruesome, gaping wound. It will require some practice, but it is well worth the effort.

You Will Need:

- make-up – red blusher and foundation that matches your skin tone
- make-up brushes
- make-up remover
- a sachet of unflavoured gelatin
- a lolly stick
- red food colouring
- a tablespoon of cornflour
- cotton buds
- a tissue
- a cup of hot water

WHAT YOU DO

1. First, clean the area of skin that you want to create your scar on (it is easiest to practise on your leg). Use make-up remover to get rid of any oil or grease. Pat dry with a tissue.

2. Mix half a cup of hot water with a sachet of unflavoured gelatin. Stir with a lolly stick until the mixture is syrupy. Allow it to cool a little so it won't burn your skin, then apply a layer to your skin in a rectangle about 7 centimetres by 5 centimetres. Let this layer dry on your skin, then apply a second layer over the same area. (Don't leave the gelatin in the cup too long as it will set and be too difficult to apply to your skin.)

3. Before the second layer of gelatin mix dries, draw the lolly stick across the middle of the layer to create a 'gash' down the centre. Allow this to dry. You may need to experiment, varying the depth and texture of the gelatin, to achieve a realistic-looking gash.

4. Once the mixture has set, your wound is in place and it's time to cover it with make-up so that its colour blends with your skin. Gently pat some foundation on the 'scar' and blend it all over the scar area. Be as gentle as you can so as not to dent or flatten the gelatin.

5. Now you need to apply some red blusher with a small make-up brush to make the inside of the gash appear pink and sore.

6. Create some fake blood by mixing a few drops of red food colouring with cornflour and a tablespoon of water. Use a cotton bud to dab the 'blood' at various points around the scar. Leave it to dry.

7. Stand back and admire your handiwork. Be prepared to lap up all the sympathy you will receive for your terrible injury.

Top Tip. It's a good idea to ask before you borrow anyone's make-up or you may end up with a scar for real!

HOW TO WHISTLE LOUDLY

Whistling in tune is all well and good, but sometimes you can't beat a really loud whistle to grab someone's attention or show your appreciation. Here's how you do it.

1. 'Wet your whistle' or take a drink of water. Learning to whistle loudly can be a thirsty business.

2. Use the thumb and index finger of one hand to make a 'U' shape. Leave about a half-centimetre gap between the tips. Put your fingers in your mouth.

3. Curl your lips back against your teeth and around your fingers. Leave only a tiny bit of your lips visible. Make sure they are stretched tight.

4. Press your tongue down just behind your bottom teeth. You should have a small bump in the middle of your tongue while the front of it should be wide and flat.

5. Breathe in through your nose then blow air out through the small gap in your fingers. Use the top of your tongue to guide the air. You may find that pushing down with your fingers on your bottom lip and teeth helps. Keep practising until you can position everything perfectly and adjust your breath for maximum whistling volume.

HOW TO SLACKLINE

'Slacklining' is a bit like tightrope-walking in that you can impress your friends and family by walking along a narrow line above the ground. However, unlike tightrope-walkers who walk along a taut rope or cable, slackliners walk on specially made rubber tubing or 'webbing', making it a far more exciting and bouncy activity.

First you need to master the technique of setting up a slackline properly. Your local sports shop or leisure centre should be able to help you get hold of the equipment you need.

You Will Need:

• three karabiners (these are metal rock-climbing clips with a spring-loaded gate) • two short pieces of slackline or webbing (3.5 m long and at least 20 mm wide) • one long length of slackline (15 m long and 20 mm wide)

SETTING UP YOUR SLACKLINE

1. Find two sturdy trees, roughly five metres apart.

2. Loop one of the short lines (line 1) around one of the trees about half a metre above the ground. Holding the two ends of this line together and using them as if they were one piece, knot them to a karabiner (A) using a clove hitch (you can learn how to tie a clove hitch on page 28 of this book).

Using the same technique, loop the other short line (line 2) around the second tree and knot it to a karabiner (B) using another clove hitch.

3. Go back to the first tree and knot the long, main line (line 3) to karabiner A using another clove hitch.

4. Now carry the other end of line 3 back towards the other tree. At a point roughly 30 centimetres away from karabiner B, knot a third karabiner (C) to line 3 using another clove hitch.

CREATING A PULLEY SYSTEM

5. Now you need to make a pulley system to control the tension on your main line. To do this, thread line 3 through karabiner B. Then loop the line back through the karabiner C.

6. Now make a double loop by looping line 3 again through karabiner B and then through karabiner C. Make sure this second loop fits inside the first loop that you made. Loosely tie the end of line 3 to karabiner C to hold your pulley system in place.

7. Before you come to walk on your slackline untie line 3 from karabiner C and pull gently on the end of this line. When your line is taut enough to walk on, tie the loose bit of line 3 back to karabiner C to hold it in place. Experiment with different levels of tautness until you find a level that you are comfortable walking on – if the line is too loose it will lose its bouncy quality when you walk on it. If you have set it up correctly, your slackline should look like this:

first tree   second tree

WALK WITH CONFIDENCE

Ask an adult to check your slackline is secure. Now it's time to learn how to walk the line.

Start in the middle of the line rather than at an end. Get two friends to stand either side of the line to support you. Grip the line between the big toe and second toe of each foot – you need to walk barefoot to help you grip.

Keep your head level and always look forwards, not down. Attempt to balance yourself on the line. Focus on balancing from your hips rather than any other part of the body.

Put your arms out at shoulder level as though you are imitating a plane – this will steady you a little. However, don't expect the line to be still. It will wobble when you are standing on it – this is what slacklining is all about. The trick is to let your body move with the movement of the line. If you resist the bounce, you are more likely to fall off.

To start walking, keep your weight on your right leg. Carefully move your left leg out and forwards until your left foot is resting comfortably on the line. Then, transfer your weight on to it.

Get your balance, then take the next step in the same way. You are now slacklining!

HOW TO STOP YOUR TRAINERS STINKING

It takes a lot of skill and effort to make sure your trainers have that lived-in 'street' look. The last thing you want is your mum threatening to undo your hard work by washing them, or throwing them in the bin because they're ponging out the house. A few simple steps mean you can have trainers that look good on the outside and smell good on the inside.

- **Bicarbonate Of Soda.** Put a teaspoon of this in each trainer and shake it around. Leave overnight then shake out into the bin.

- **Old Socks.** Fill a pair of old, clean socks with some cat litter (clean cat litter, of course). Stick a sock in each trainer and leave them overnight.

- **Tea Leaves.** Try putting loose tea into each trainer. Shake it all out in the morning.

HOW TO BE A VENTRILOQUIST

Ventriloquists use their voices and their powers of illusion to bring a dummy to 'life'. To become a good ventriloquist you will need to convince an audience that the dummy is talking, not you. Here are some basic skills you need to master.

DON'T MOVE YOUR LIPS

It's almost impossible to speak without moving your lips at all, so don't worry if you struggle with this. However, it is important to restrict your lip movements as much as possible.

Sit in front of a mirror and hold a finger to your lips as if making a 'shushing' gesture. Say the sounds of the alphabet out loud. You will notice that some letters make your lips move more than others. The worst offenders are usually 'b', 'p', 'm' and 'w'.

What you have to do is substitute these letters with similar sounds that won't make your lips move so much. Now, try saying 'd' for 'b', 'kl' for 'p', 'n' for 'm' and 'ooh' for 'w'.

This will sound odd at first, but keep practising and you'll find that you are able to slip these substitutes into words without other people noticing.

DON'T BE A DUMMY!

A ventriloquist's dummy is vital to the success of an act. It distracts the audience's attention from your mouth by looking and sounding funny.

You can use anything from an old doll to a well-loved teddy bear as your dummy. However, a sock puppet (a sock with two eyes sewn on it and a 'mouth' operated by your thumb in the toe of the sock) is great to practise with, as you can get used to moving the dummy's mouth in time with the words you are speaking.

CHANGE YOUR VOICE

Don't forget that the trick to ventriloquism is to fool your audience into thinking that your dummy is talking, not you. One of the ways to do this is to give your dummy a voice that is different to your own, so practise changing the tone and the speed at which you usually talk. Always practise in front of a mirror so you can check how visible your lip movements are.

HOW TO BE A FROTHING-FOAM FIGHTER

Water fights are fantastically wet fun, but imagine a foam fight that ensures everyone gets the frothiest of soakings.

You Will Need:

- a lot of space (preferably a garden or a park)
- some large plastic bottles (lids removed)
- washing-up liquid • baking soda • vinegar • warm water

1. Add a good squeeze of washing-up liquid to your plastic bottle. Then fill it three-quarters full with warm water. Add two teaspoons of baking soda.

2. Put your hand over the top of the bottle and give it a good shake so the liquid starts bubbling up. (Never screw on the lid as this can be dangerous – and explosive!)

3. Add a final magic ingredient – a teaspoon of vinegar. The bubble mixture in each bottle should magically turn to foam.

4. Squeeze your bottle to shoot out the foam. Take aim and let the foam fight begin.

Warning. Avoid squirting foam in your opponent's eyes at all times.

HOW TO 'POP-UP' ON A SURFBOARD

The key to standing up successfully on a surfboard is learning the 'pop-up' manoeuvre. This is the basic move that helps you get to your feet on your board as quickly and smoothly as possible.

The best place to practise 'popping-up' on your surfboard is on dry land. Learning on an unstable surface like a floating surfboard is only likely to take you in one direction – under the water. So, instead of risking constant duckings, practise on dry land. Take your surfboard, remove the fins (which are usually detachable) and lie it flat on the beach, on the grass in your garden or even on the floor of your bedroom.

WHAT YOU DO

1. Lie flat on your board. Begin by doing a press-up – pushing your body upwards by straightening your arms.

2. Once your arms are straight, jump your legs and feet forwards, bringing your knees towards your chest, so you are in a crouching position. If you are right-handed, your right foot should be slightly in front of your left foot.

3. Straighten your legs so you are standing in a sideways position with your feet apart. Your right foot should be near the middle of the board, the other towards the tail.

KEEP PRACTISING

Don't stand too upright or lean backwards – you're liable to fall over if you do. Instead, try and keep both legs slightly bent. Lean forwards a little, and use your arms to help you balance.

If you are struggling to get to your feet, straighten your arms, and with both your knees pulled up towards your stomach, slide your front foot towards the nose of your board.

Keep practising this move until you can do it in one smooth movement. Once you have mastered how to pop-up, take your board out onto the water and try catching some waves for real.

HOW TO CATCH A WAVE

Before you can impress everyone with your smooth skills on a surfboard, you need to learn the basic principles of catching a wave.

Grab your board and follow the steps below – you'll soon be catching waves all the way in to shore.

WHAT YOU DO

1. When you are waist-deep in the water, lie face down on your board and start paddling out to sea. As you reach the point where waves are breaking, shift your weight forwards to lower the front of your board and paddle fast, ducking under the breaking waves. This is called 'duck-diving'. You are aiming to pass the place where the waves are breaking to where they are starting to form a swell.

2. Once you're in position, stop paddling and sit astride your board slightly nearer the back than the front. Wait until you spot a wave that is big enough or travelling fast enough to pick you up and carry you all the way to shore.

3. As the wave approaches, turn and point your board towards the shore. Lie flat on it and start to paddle. Don't let your body get too close to the nose of your board as you may push it underwater. As you feel the wave lifting and pushing you towards the shore, paddle as fast as you can.

4. As the wave carries you forward, stop paddling. To keep your board moving as fast as possible, raise your chest a little to shift your weight backwards. However, do not lean back too far, as this will slow you down.

5. Once you've caught a few waves, you're ready to begin standing up on your surfboard using the pop-up move you learnt on pages 67 and 68.

Warnings. Only go in the sea if you can see a red and yellow flag flying on the beach – this means there is a trained lifeguard on the beach and it is safe to swim. Keep to the area between the flags.

Always, make sure you take care to stay out of the way of other surfers if the water is busy. They will not be pleased if you cut in on their wave.

Never go surfing alone, and be sure to return to the beach before it gets dark.

Do not go into the water if there are signs saying 'No swimming', a red flag or a warning of strong currents.

HOW TO RIDE A WAVE

Once you've mastered catching waves and popping-up on your surfboard, you need to learn how to ride a wave.

Surfing standing up is all about riding along the front of a wave, staying parallel to the beach. This allows you to surf faster and for longer. It takes a lot of practice, but here are some top tips.

- Once the wave has begun to carry you forwards, pop-up to get you on your feet.

- To keep going as fast as possible, you need to travel along the unbroken part of a wave (not the whitewater). To do this you will need to steer your board in the right direction. Begin by keeping your body low – bending your legs and adopting a crouching stance. Position your front foot in the direction you want to travel and lean your weight slightly onto this foot.

- Try to keep most of your body weight over the middle of the board – this will help stop you from falling off.

- Focus your eyes on the part of the wave you want to ride.

You're surfing!

HOW TO CALL LIKE TARZAN

Everyone knows that Tarzan is King of the Jungle, famous for wrestling crocodiles and swinging from trees. But he is most famous for his amazing jungle call. Here's how you can recreate Tarzan's distinctive call and perhaps even summon animals.

Find somewhere you can practise without disturbing your friends and neighbours (it might be best to make sure you're not close to a zoo, just in case). Fill your lungs with air, then make an 'ahhhh' sound from the back of your throat.

After a couple of seconds, gently beat the top of your chest with your fists. This will cause your voice to change, creating a yodelling effect. Beating different areas of your chest will make different sounds.

Try to maintain the call for at least ten seconds, and vary it by changing the flow of your breath.

HOW TO BE A DARING DARTS PLAYER

Hanging a darts board on your bedroom wall and practising your throwing technique will get you hitting the bullseye in no time.

Follow these essential tips on how to become a darts champion.

GET A GRIP

Different players grip the shaft of a dart in different ways, so you will need to experiment to find the grip that is most comfortable. However, all grips follow the same principles:

1. Hold the dart with your thumb on one side and two fingers on the other. Keep your other fingers folded well out of the way.

2. Keep the grip on your dart light. If your fingers show any whiteness at the tips, your grip is too tight. Too much pressure will make it harder to throw the dart cleanly.

3. Hold your dart straight and parallel to the floor at all times. Never point it down or up.

BODY POSITIONING

Your body position is important, too. Stand slightly sideways to the board with your throwing arm closest to it. Place one foot in front of the other. Your leading foot (the same side as your throwing arm) should be at right angles to the 'oche' (the line behind which players stand to throw their darts). Position your other foot behind to balance you, but keep your weight over the leading foot.

YOUR RELEASE

Aim your dart at the board, concentrating on the spot you want to hit. Bend your arm. Then extend your arm so that it is straight. When your arm is fully extended release the dart by snapping your wrist. Only your shooting arm should move. Your shoulder should stay completely still.

At the end of your release, your throwing fingers should be pointing down in the direction of the floor.

Keep the release movement smooth. Don't spin the dart by rolling it through your fingers.

If you find the weight of your body falling to one side after you have released the dart, your body isn't balanced correctly. Close your eyes and try to hit the bullseye with a dart. Shutting your eyes will help you with your balance as you will be able to feel more clearly which parts of your body are moving.

BULLSEYE!

Once your release is going well, you are ready to start playing a game of darts.

Get a friend to play with you. Each player begins with 301 points. Take it in turns to throw three darts at the board. After each round count up how many points you have scored and subtract the total from 301.

Keep subtracting until one player is able to reduce their score to zero. The first person to reach zero wins the game.

HOW TO FAKE A SPILT DRINK

Here is an excellent practical joke that will temporarily cause panic at the dinner table.

You Will Need:

• a paper cup • PVA glue • orange food colouring
• an old plastic bag • scissors

WHAT YOU DO

1. Take a cup and pour in about a tablespoon of PVA glue. Add a few drops of orange food colouring to create the look of spilled orange juice. Stir.

2. Spread the plastic bag out on a flat surface. Tip the cup on one side and dribble glue out of the cup to make the shape of a liquid spill on the plastic bag. Make sure the cup is resting on the plastic bag and touching the edge of the 'spill'. Leave the glue to set.

3. Once the glue is dry, cut around your spill with scissors.

Wait until the table is laid for a special occasion, then position your spill. You might need earplugs for when your trick is discovered.

HOW TO POWER A LIGHT BULB WITH A LEMON

Everyone talks about green power, but here's a little 'yellow' power. Read on to discover how you can turn on a light bulb with a lemon.

You Will Need:

- a large, fresh lemon • a zinc screw about 5 cm long
- a copper screw about 5 cm long • a set of old Christmas tree lights • a pair of pliers

WHAT YOU DO

1. First of all, you need to get the juice flowing inside the lemon by gently squeezing or rolling it on a hard surface. Don't break the skin – you don't want any juice to escape.

copper screw

zinc screw

2. Screw the zinc screw into one side of the lemon and the copper screw into the opposite side. Don't screw them all the way through, and don't allow them to touch each other in the middle. You are aiming to leave them so that the ends of the nails are about 2 centimetres apart inside the lemon.

3. Use the pliers to snip one of the Christmas tree light bulbs off from the set. Make sure you leave about 5 centimetres of wire on either side of the base of the bulb. Ask an adult for help with this.

copper screw

zinc screw

4. Now carefully peel away about 2.5 centimetres of the plastic insulation from the light's wires to expose the metal wires beneath.

5. Once the end of each wire is exposed, wrap one bare end around the zinc screw.

6. Dim the lights in the room and close the curtains or blinds. Quickly wrap the bare end of the other wire around the copper screw.

7. Look carefully and you'll see that the bulb has been illuminated by the lemon-yellow power. The acid in the lemon juice creates a chemical reaction when it touches the metal, producing energy. This energy is enough to light the bulb.

HOW TO SKID YOUR BIKE

Skidding the back wheel of your bike, also known as a 'Side Skid', is a simple but effective stunt you can do with just a little practice. It makes for a pretty impressive entrance.

BEFORE YOU START

- Your bike should be in good condition, with the tyres pumped up and with good treads on them.

- Your brakes should be working well, and you must wear safety gear, such as elbow and knee pads and a helmet.

- You need a hard surface for skidding, so choose an unused stretch of tarmac or a concrete area in a playground. Make sure there are no other vehicles using the area before you attempt a skid.

PERFORMING A SIDE SKID

1. Start by pedalling fairly slowly, travelling roughly the same speed as a slow jog. Don't worry if this seems a bit slow – once you've mastered the technique, you can go faster.

2. Move your weight forwards off the back wheel and lean slightly to the right as if you're about to go round a corner.

3. Take your right foot off the pedal, and hold it straight out to the side. Keep it just above the ground. Then brake hard with your back brake (the back brake is usually operated by the brake on the left-hand side of your handlebars, but it can vary).

4. You should feel the back tyre trying to grip the ground, and the bike will begin to rotate, skidding to the left. As your bike comes to a standstill, put your right foot down to steady yourself.

5. Practise the side skid, building up your speed gradually, for a more impressive and longer-lasting skid.

HOW TO WIN A BET

The next time you want to win a bet with your best mate, why not try this trick?

You Will Need:

- 500 g of cornflour • water • a large mixing bowl
- a pound coin • a wristwatch or stopwatch

WHAT YOU DO

1. Pour the cornflour into the bowl. Slowly add some water and stir the mixture until you get a thick, custard-like consistency.

2. Invite your friend into the kitchen and show him the mixture.

3. Ask him to give you a pound coin and find one of your own. Drop both coins into the bowl.

4. Now challenge your friend to put his hand in and grab one coin within five seconds. If he manages it, he can keep both coins. If he doesn't, you will keep them.

5. Time five seconds and see how he gets on.

THE VICTORY

You will find that the quicker your friend attempts to grab the money, the faster and harder the mixture will set around his hand. This should make it impossible to fish out either of the coins.

To show him how it is done, put your hand into the mix very s-l-o-w-l-y, find a coin and slowly take it out.

Top Tip. Practise your technique beforehand to get your time down to five seconds or less. Remember, the slower your hand moves around in the mixture, the easier it will be to fish out the coin.

HOW TO GO CRABBING

Crabbing's a great thing to do if you're on holiday by the sea or a tidal river. It's easy to master and you can normally catch crabs without a lot of specialist knowledge or fancy equipment.

You Will Need:

- a piece of string or fishing line • a metal hook (the top of a wire coat hanger would work) • a nut or bolt
- some uncooked bacon to use as bait
- a bucket • a small fishing net

WHAT YOU DO

1. To make your crabbing line, tie the hook to the end of your string or fishing line. Tie the nut or bolt to the line directly above the hook to weigh the line down.

2. Find a good spot for crabbing – beside a harbour wall, bridge, floating jetty or pontoon. Unlike fish, there are usually plenty of crabs to go round, so you don't need to find an isolated spot.

3. Fill your bucket with water from the sea or tidal river – you can put some bacon in it if you have some spare.

4. Bait the hook on the end of your crabbing line with some bacon. (Rinse your hands thoroughly after handling the bait.)

5. Drop your baited hook into the water and let it sink to the bottom, keeping a tight hold of your end of the line. Wait for a few moments for your weight to settle on the bottom.

6. Wait patiently until you feel a slight tug on the line. Then bring your line up slowly until you can see if anything is on the end. If you've been successful, it will have a crab clinging on to it. Reach down with your fishing net and transfer the crab from the hook into your bucket of water.

Remember that crabs are living, feeling creatures. You should always treat them gently and lower them back to where they came from once you have caught them. Don't throw them back as this might hurt them, and don't leave them on the shore where birds may eat them.

Top Tip. See how many crabs you can catch, or have a race with your friend to see who can catch the most in a set period of time – say twenty minutes.

HOW TO BE A JIGSAW GENIUS

It's Christmas and your house is full of relatives. Someone empties thousands of tiny pieces of a particularly puzzling jigsaw puzzle onto the floor, and challenges you to complete the picture. If you don't want to be sitting still solving the puzzle on New Year's Eve, you need to follow the steps below.

1. Give yourself enough room to take every piece of the jigsaw out of the box.

2. Prop up the picture you are aiming to complete close to you. This is the biggest clue to helping you solve the puzzle, so make sure you can see it clearly.

3. Separate out all the pieces with one or two flat surfaces. These will form the edge of the picture.

4. Build the border of the picture first (this is usually rectangular), using up all the edge pieces you have found. This will allow you to get an idea of the shape and size of the puzzle.

5. Place all the remaining jigsaw pieces outside of the edge you've just put together – this will stop you getting confused.

6. Now group together pieces which are a similar colour. Refer to the picture and work out which areas of the picture these pieces might belong to. They might be sky, cloud or water, for example.

7. Collect together pieces that are distinctive – for example parts of a bright red car or a yellow boat. Start building this section of the puzzle.

8. If you get stuck, look at the picture for any outlines, lines or shapes that link several pieces. These might include windows in a building or something like a zebra crossing or pavement edge on an outdoor scene. Start building this section.

9. Signs or wording are usually easy to pick out, so focus on finding these pieces. They should be easy to put together and place in the approximate position within the border.

10. Don't get discouraged. If you are getting really bogged down, try grouping the remaining pieces into groups of similar shapes. Then, if you know the shape that a piece has to be, you can try out all the correctly-shaped pieces one by one, until one fits. Good luck!

Top Tip. Take regular breaks from working on the puzzle. Often if you return to a puzzle a bit later, you will immediately spot the missing piece you thought you would never find.

HOW TO MAKE AN EDIBLE IGLOO

How come there is never enough snow to build a real igloo? Get some practice by building one out of sugar cubes instead of blocks of snow. Your hands won't get so cold and you could always feed it to a horse when you're finished.

You Will Need:

• a box of sugar cubes • a circle of cardboard 15 cm in diameter • 500 g of royal icing sugar • three tablespoons of water • greaseproof paper

BUILDING YOUR IGLOO

1. To start, build the bottom row of your igloo by placing sugar cubes around the edge of the circle of card. Make some icing paste by mixing together the icing sugar and water. Then spread the paste on the side of each cube like cement, before you add it to the existing structure. Don't forget to leave room for the entrance.

2. Now start building around and upwards, adding a layer of icing paste on top of every cube. Stop for about 20 minutes after each row is completed to allow it to dry. You should be aiming to build up about eight layers of sugar cubes. Stagger the cubes, making each row a slightly smaller circle than the last.

3. Make the entrance arch and flat roof section of the igloo separately. Build them on a flat surface, lined with greaseproof paper, to prevent them from sticking to the surface you are working on. Let them harden for a good few hours until they are completely dry. Then peel them off the greaseproof paper.

4. Once you have applied the top layer of icing paste to the unfinished igloo, carefully position the arch, adding some more icing paste to fix it in place. Now gently place the roof on top of the other layers. Leave to dry.

5. Pop your igloo on a plate. For a finishing touch, sprinkle it with sugar snow (icing sugar) and decorate with Arctic figures. An edible igloo makes a great Christmas decoration, so why not give it to your mum when you're finished with it?

HOW TO SAVE A PENALTY

You're in goal and a penalty is awarded against your team. Don't panic. If you don't save the penalty, everyone will understand, but if you do – you're a hero. Here's how you can become a team legend.

- The rules say you are not allowed to move off the goal line before the ball is struck by the person taking the penalty. So jump up and down on the spot with your arms and legs spread wide apart. This will make you as big a target as possible and hopefully put the striker off.

- Watch the striker's body language as he prepares to take the shot. Look carefully to see if his eyes give away which corner of the goal he intends to aim the ball at.

- Watch to see if the striker is nervous or confident. If he is nervous he is likely to hesitate or make a weak shot. If he is confident he will probably try to show off by hitting it over your head. If you know it's coming, get ready to jump high to save the ball.

- If the striker is right-footed, he is likely to strike the right side of the ball. This will mean the ball will be aimed towards the centre of the net or to the left-hand side, so aim your dive accordingly.

- Always, always dive. Even if the ball is blasted down the middle, you may save it with your legs or feet. Dive just before the ball is struck. It will be travelling so fast that if you dive after the ball is hit, it will be in the net before you have any chance of making a save.

With a bit of luck you will leave the pitch as the 'Man of the Match'!

HOW TO AVOID LIGHTNING STRIKES

You're walking to the shops on a sunny day and suddenly the sky darkens and a thunderstorm is unleashed. Follow this essential advice to stay safe:

- As soon as you see a flash of lightning, start counting. Count how many seconds it is before you hear the thunder (saying the word 'elephant' between each number you count will help you be more accurate). Take the number of seconds and divide it by three. This gives you a very approximate indication of how many kilometres away from you the storm is.

- If thunder follows the lightning by less than 20 seconds then you are near the centre of the storm and it is time to act.

- Avoid sheds, open-top cars, trees, flagpoles or mobile communication masts. If possible, get inside a large, enclosed building.

- Once inside, stay away from the telephone, water taps and electrical appliances such as the TV or computer. These items act as 'conductors' and the lightning's electric charge can travel through them. If you touch a conductor that has been struck by lightning, the electric current produced will then flow into you. So stay well away from them!

- If you can't get safely inside, and are in an exposed area such as a field or beach, here's what to do. Remove any metal objects, such as watches, rings or necklaces, and throw them away from you – these too can act as conductors. Kneel down, placing your fingers, knees and toes on the ground. Bend your head low to the ground and wait for the storm to pass.

HOW TO BE A SOUND-EFFECTS WIZARD

A sound-effects engineer can play tricks with your ears by creating a convincing sound to accompany an action. If they have done their job well, you will not suspect any deception has taken place.

It's a great job – but have you got what it takes to become a sound-effects wizard? A real sound-effects engineer will have a range of complex electronic equipment at his fingertips and a studio to work from, but you don't need either of these. The key to producing great sound effects is being creative and using whatever is around you to create the noise that you need.

Here are some convincing sound effects you can generate using simple everyday objects. Try some of the following stunts on your friends and family and see if they fall for your sound effects.

- Complain to your mum that your finger is hurting so much that you are determined to saw it off. Disappear from view (but stay within earshot), and saw a raw cabbage in half with a serrated knife (one with a jagged edge). This will produce the desired hair-raising sound and your mum will soon come running.

- You are out in the garden, when you and a friend spot a huge beetle walking along the ground. As you're friend looks away, pretend to step on the beetle (make sure you don't actually harm the beetle by mistake). As you step, scrunch a bag of potato crisps hidden behind your back. Your friend will believe you have actually trodden on the beetle if you have done it successfully.

- Your mum hands you an important letter to drop in the postbox on your way to school. As your mum turns away, bring the edge of the letter up to your lips and blow hard – so your breath rushes along the front and back of the letter. At the same time move your hands as if you are tearing something in two. If you get it right, the sound you make should be the same as if you had ripped the letter in half. Wait for the look on your mum's face.

- Complain to your dad that your kid brother or sister is annoying you. Move so you are standing directly between your dad's line of vision and your sibling, then turn and slap your own forearm sharply. Your dad will be convinced you have whacked your brother/sister.

- For an embarrassing sound, as your friend sits down in a chair, rub your hand across an inflated, wet balloon – the effect is very funny indeed!

HOW TO TELL A GOOD JOKE

Q. What is the king of the hankies called?

A. The 'hanki'–chief!

OK, so that joke's not likely to bring the house down, but some people are able to tell any joke and get their audience to laugh. How? By following these dos and don'ts.

DO

- DO know your joke back-to-front and inside out. How many times have people started to tell you a joke then stopped because they can't remember the story or the punchline?

• DO pace yourself. Never rush through your joke. Be confident and enjoy telling it. Your audience will share your enjoyment and be more inclined to laugh at the end.

• DO keep your jokes fairly short. It's very hard to hold an audience's concentration for more than two minutes.

• DO be confident. Keep your delivery lively.

• DO make the punchline strong. Try to stay confident right through to the end of the joke. Your audience is waiting patiently for the killer ending that will make them roar with laughter, so don't let them down by fluffing the punchline.

• DO build up a collection of good jokes. Copy any joke that makes you laugh from friends or professionals, and adapt them to suit you.

DON'T

• DON'T try to tell jokes in strange accents unless you can do them really well. At best, your accent might confuse the audience. At worst, it might offend people.

• DON'T tell just any joke. Choose one that suits your audience and their interests.

• DON'T be put off if your audience doesn't like your jokes. Listen to which bits they do laugh at and next time leave out the bits that got groaned at or booed.

HOW TO BEAT THE CLOCK WHEN YOU GET UP

You never know when you might need to get dressed in a hurry. Next time you've slept through your alarm, these tips will save you valuable seconds.

- **Choose Your Clothes The Night Before.** Everyone's a bit slow and sleepy in the morning, so choose what you're going to wear when you're wide awake – and save time rooting around in your wardrobe while you're half-asleep.

- **Take Your Clothes Off Carefully.** If you have to wear a shirt and tie for school, loosen your tie but keep it knotted and hanging around your shirt collar. Undo the top two buttons of the shirt, keeping everything together. Tomorrow you can pop both over your head in a hurry.

- **Keep Layers Intact.** If you're wearing a T-shirt and jumper, always pull both off at the same time – not one by one. That way you will be able to pull them on again all in one go tomorrow morning.

- **Put Out Your Socks And Underwear.** This will ensure you don't leave the house with one red sock and one blue sock on.

- **Keep Some Clothes On.** If it's cold, just keep your socks on at night. That's one less thing to do tomorrow!

HOW TO BE A KUNG-FU KING

One of the most famous moves in kung fu is the 'High Kick'. Practise in front of a mirror or try kicking a cushion suspended at chest height. This will allow you to improve the speed, power and accuracy of your kick.

Here's how you can sharpen your kicking skills in this vital area:

• Stand at a 45° angle to your target. Position the leg you are going to kick with just behind your hips and the other leg just in front. Seventy per cent of your weight should be resting on your back leg.

• Transfer your weight forward on to your front foot, keeping your back as straight as possible. As you do, lift your kicking leg with the knee bent. Pivot on your front foot so your raised knee is pointing directly at your target. Lift the knee as high as you can (at least as high as your waist).

• You are aiming to hit your target with the top part of your foot. Do this by straightening your leg rapidly in a kicking motion.

• Once you have made contact, quickly return to your starting position.

Warning. Never aim a High Kick at anyone, except in self-defence.

HOW TO GET IN AND OUT OF A HAMMOCK

Hammocks are brilliant things to have in your garden and make the perfect place to relax and swing gently in the shade.

Unfortunately, getting in and out of a hammock can be the very opposite of relaxing. It's easy to end up flat on your bottom and red in the face. So follow these expert tips to make sure you stay cool at all times.

GETTING IN

Grip both sides of the hammock and pull the middle area of the cloth taut.

Don't jump on. Instead, lower your bottom onto the area you are holding taut. Rest your weight on your bottom, then lean back slightly, keeping your feet on the ground.

Once your back is on the hammock, slowly swing your legs off the ground and into the hammock.

Try and lie at a slight angle with your head at one side of the hammock and your feet diagonally across it at the other side.

GETTING OUT

When you've woken up or it's time to get out of your hammock, the first thing to do is turn onto your side.

Slowly move your legs over the edge of the hammock and lower them until they are touching the ground.

Hold on to the front edge of the hammock with both hands.

As you transfer your weight from the hammock to your feet, push the hammock away from underneath you.

If you've timed it right, you should find yourself on your feet with the hammock swinging away from you.

HOW TO RECOGNISE DEADLY SNAKES

If you're travelling to a different country or another part of your own country that is known for its venomous snakes, it's a good idea to be able to recognise what some experts consider the top five deadliest snakes in the world.

If you do come across one, stay calm and try and move slowly out of the snake's range. If you are bitten, get medical help immediately. Being able to identify the snake that bit you may just save your life as it will help the paramedics decide which antivenom you need. Carefully read the descriptions of each snake below.

THE INLAND TAIPAN (ALSO KNOWN AS THE FIERCE SNAKE)

Found In: Dry, arid regions of Australia.
Deadly Rating: 1st. This snake's venom is the deadliest in the world. Just one milligrame of its venom is fatal to a human being.
Nature: Generally inactive but will attack if provoked.
Appearance: These snakes can grow up to 1.7 metres long. The back, sides and tail are often pale brown in colour, but the rest of the body is usually black in winter and dark brown in summer.

THE AUSTRALIAN BROWN SNAKE (ALSO KNOWN AS THE COMMON EASTERN BROWN SNAKE)

Found In: Australia, Indonesia and Papua New Guinea.

Deadly Rating: 2nd. This snake is responsible for more deaths in Australia than any other.

Nature: Aggressive.

Appearance: These snakes can grow up to almost 2 metres long. They are mostly brown and can have a range of patterns on their backs, including multi-coloured bands and speckles. They can move very fast across the ground. When angry, they hold their necks high in an S-shape.

THE MALAYAN KRAIT (ALSO KNOWN AS THE BLUE KRAIT)

Found In: Southeast Asia.

Deadly Rating: 3rd. The Malayan krait's venom is fifteen times stronger than a cobra's.

Nature: Timid during the day. More aggressive at night.

Appearance: This snake can grow up to 1.5 metres in length. Its back has black and white bands that widen as they reach its white underside. The head is greyish, with lighter lips. This snake will often hide its head within its coiled body for protection.

THE TIGER SNAKE

Found In: Southern Australia, Tasmania and its coastal islands.
Deadly Rating: 4th.
If untreated, more than half of bites are fatal.
Nature: Aggressive if threatened.

Appearance: Tiger snakes grow to about 1.5 metres long. They often have bands, like a tiger, but range in colour from yellow and black to olive- and orange-brown with a paler underside. If threatened, tiger snakes make a loud hissing noise and will raise their heads like a cobra to strike.

THE SAW-SCALED VIPER

Found In: The Middle East, Central Asia, India and surrounding areas.
Deadly Rating: 5th.
These vipers are responsible for more human deaths than any other species of snake.
Nature: Aggressive and quick-tempered.

Appearance: They grow to about 1 metre long, and have short pear-shaped heads, with quite large eyes. The scales on their lower sides stick out at an angle of 45°. When threatened, they form C-shaped coils and rub their coils together, making a loud sizzling noise. They move quickly with a side-winding action.

HOW TO TALK LIKE A PILOT

If you've ever listened in on a pilot's conversation, you'll know they use a special system to spell out words. It's known as the 'spoken phonetic alphabet' and is used to avoid confusion during intercom conversations. Learn the alphabet below off by heart so you can use it in emergency situations or when it is vital you are understood.

A – Alpha	H – Hotel	O – Oscar	V – Victor
B – Bravo	I – India	P – Papa	W – Whisky
C – Charlie	J – Juliet	Q – Quebec	X – X-ray
D – Delta	K – Kilo	R – Romeo	Y – Yankee
E – Echo	L – Lima	S – Sierra	Z – Zulu
F – Foxtrot	M – Mike	T – Tango	
G – Golf	N – November	U – Uniform	

Here are a few useful words that might come in handy:

That's a super-large, deep crust, mega Papa India Zulu Zulu Alpha please.

Mayday – 'Help!'
Roger, Over and Out – Ends a conversation.
Ten-Four – Confirms you have understood the message.
Sit-rep – Stands for 'situation report', such as 'where are you?', 'is anybody injured?' etc.

101

HOW TO LOOK AROUND CORNERS

How do you look round corners or make sure you get the best view in the cinema when the biggest kid in town is sitting in front of you? Easy – bring your own periscope.

You Will Need:

• two cardboard juice cartons (wash them out and let them dry before using them) • a marker pen • scissors • a ruler • strong tape • two small rectangular-shaped mirrors

WHAT YOU DO

1. Carefully cut the top off each juice carton, so each one is squared off.

2. Cut a rectangular opening at the bottom of one of your cartons. Leave about one centimetre of carton around the sides and bottom of the hole you have just made.

3. Place the carton on its side with the hole facing you. Lie your mirror flat on top of the carton so that its longer side aligns with the bottom. Mark a spot at the bottom right-hand and top left-hand corner of the mirror with a pen. Remove the mirror and use your ruler to draw a diagonal line to join the two dots, as shown.

4. Cut along the line you have drawn. Then slide the mirror through this slot. Turn the carton round and look through the hole you've already cut in the front of the carton. You should be able to see the sawn-off top section of the carton in the mirror. Use tape to fix the mirror in place.

5. Now do exactly the same with the other juice carton.

Look through here.

6. Turn one of the cartons upside down and place it on top of the other one. A square opening should be at the bottom facing you and another at the top facing away from you. If you've got everything aligned correctly, you should be able to look through the bottom opening and see what's ahead of you. Stick the two cartons together with tape.

Congratulations, you have made a periscope. You will find that what is ahead of you is reflected in the upper mirror, and then reflected in the lower mirror. Hold it horizontally to look around corners, or hold it vertically to look over walls and fences.

HOW TO ROLL A KAYAK

Performing a roll involves capsizing your kayak and then rolling yourself back to the surface in one fluid movement. This roll is a tribute to the skill and mastery displayed by the Inuit people in the Arctic Circle when out fishing in their kayak. Read on to find out how to perform this manoeuvre.

Warning. Never attempt to roll a kayak on your own. Always learn to use a kayak with an instructor or as part of a supervised class. Wear all the appropriate safety gear, including a helmet and life jacket.

WHAT YOU DO

Hold your paddle out of the water on the left-hand side of the kayak. Lean forwards at the waist so that you are lying low and tight against the front of the kayak.

Now, tip your body over to the left side of the kayak, so that you and the kayak roll under the surface of the water.

THE SWEEP

As soon as your body is underwater, lean to your left side again to tip the kayak back towards the surface. Sweep the outboard blade of your paddle (the curved part of the blade nearest your

right hand) in a full arc through the water, pushing back and away from the kayak's side. The 'Sweep' will help you roll the kayak while you are underwater, so that you are almost at the surface again.

104

THE HIP SNAP

To bring your body all the way out of the water and your kayak the right way up, you will need to perform a 'Hip Snap'.

The first part of the Hip Snap involves rocking the kayak to your left and then back again to your right. To do this, first stretch your waist all the way to your left. Then quickly stretch your waist all the way to your right. To complete the Hip Snap, jut your hip towards your right side at the last moment and you should reach the surface with enough force to snap the kayak out of the water.

Your head and body should be underwater at all times when performing the Hip Snap – if your head reaches the surface before your kayak, your kayak will drag you back down underwater.

THE RECOVERY

The momentum of the Hip Snap should pop you out of the water. Don't try and lead with your head and shoulders, as this will strain your muscles and may push you over again.

Once you're upright, take a quick stroke forwards with your paddle. This will help you reposition yourself properly in the kayak.

HOW TO SURVIVE A FLOOD

If you live or are holidaying in an area that is coastal or low-lying, with a history of flooding, a flood could potentially happen at any time. It is vital that you are prepared.

EMERGENCY KIT

Keep an emergency kit close at hand, stored somewhere that is accessible and above floodwater levels.

Your emergency kit should be sealed in a waterproof container and should include:

- drinking water in sealed bottles • a medical kit
- maps of the area • signalling devices (including a torch and a mobile phone) • a spare set of clothes • a sleeping bag or blankets • sealed plastic wallets to keep your passport and any other important documents safe

PREPARATION

Advance notice of a flood or approaching tidal wave could mean the difference between life and death, so make sure you follow news bulletins on the radio and TV.

On the first day of a holiday you should familiarise yourself with the area in which you are staying. You need to establish a prearranged meeting place on high ground or in a tall, well-constructed building. Make sure that all the members of your family know a route out of the holiday complex that will take them to your prearranged meeting place, avoiding low-lying areas, that may flood.

If possible, make sure everyone in your group carries a mobile phone at all times and that they have the number for everyone else in the group and for the emergency services.

TIME TO GO

If you are lucky enough to have advance warning of a flood, you must prepare to leave your house. Turn off all gas and electrical appliances at the mains and, if possible, move furniture and valuables upstairs.

Large objects carried in flood waters are a danger to you and other people, so lock your family's car inside the garage and bolt the door. Tie down any objects you can to stop them floating away.

Grab your emergency kit and start to make your way to your meeting place.

Never try to outrun a flood by jumping in a car and speeding off. The floodwater will move faster than you can.

Don't be tempted to cross a torrent of water that looks shallow. It is dangerous to wade through water that is any deeper than your knees. Moreover, it is very difficult to tell how strong the current is just by looking at it. The pressure of fast-flowing water on your legs can easily make you lose your balance and fall.

If you do get swept up in floodwater, try to grab something you can climb on to. While you are in the water you are at risk of being struck by debris being carried by the flood. Another potential danger in some areas of the world can be wildlife, such as snakes and crocodiles, which may be swept along in the waters, too.

HIGHER GROUND

Once you reach your meeting place, use your phone to make your position known to the emergency services. Make sure everyone with you understands how important it is to stay there until help comes.

While you wait, ration the food and water you have with you among the people you are sheltering with. Do not allow anyone to be tempted to drink from the floodwater. It will be contaminated and will probably make them sick. Use your first-aid kit to tend to anyone injured.

HOW TO SIGNAL A PLANE

If you've ever watched planes landing at an airport, you may have spotted someone in high-visibility clothing and ear protectors waving their arms at the pilot. These people are called ground controllers, and their job is to guide planes around the airport once they have safely landed.

Ground controllers communicate with pilots using a series of signals that are understood by aviators all around the world. Each signal has to be clearly executed so there is no danger of the pilot getting confused and steering his plane in the wrong direction.

Here are the ten most commonly used signals. So, next time you're at an airport, you'll know exactly what's going on.

Start engines

All clear

Normal stop

Emergency stop

Turn right

Turn left

Proceed straight ahead.

Slow down

Fire
(left arm indicates the
location of fire)

Cut engines

HOW TO MAKE THE PERFECT SNOWBALL

Making a perfect snowball is easy, right? Wrong. Anyone can create a snowball that falls apart too soon or doesn't fall apart at all, but making one that has maximum explosive effect takes skill and practice.

Perfect Temperature. The perfect time to make snowballs is when the temperature outside is around freezing. If the temperature falls below freezing, the snow gets dry and powdery and won't stick together. If this happens, try looking for snow beside your house that might be a little warmer and wetter.

If the temperature rises above freezing, the snow will be too slushy and wet. Look for snow further away from your house on an exposed area but out of direct sunlight, as this should be colder.

Lower Layers. When you locate a patch of good snow, brush off the top layer of fallen snow and use the lower levels of snow that have been packed together. This is perfect snowball-making snow.

PACKING A SNOWBALL

Compression. Start by scooping up the snow and bring your cupped hands together. As you start to press the snow together you should be able to hear the squeaking sound of the snow compressing. Don't press too hard, and stop as soon as the ball starts to feel hard.

Add one more scoop of snow and press it around the ball you have already made.

Bare hands are best to make snowballs. The heat from your body helps warm the snow so that it is easier to mould. Throwing it is the only way to truly test your creation. The perfect snowball should 'explode' on impact, leaving your target (or victim) in a cloud of snow and a tell-tale snowy imprint where the snowball hit.

Warnings. Never aim your snowballs at people's faces – this can damage their eyes.

Never throw snowballs at moving cars or anywhere near a busy road.

HOW TO PUTT LIKE A PRO

You're out on the golf course, and victory in a tournament is within your grasp – and all you have to do is sink a putt. What do you do?

DON'T RUSH

Take time to 'read' the green (the smooth, grassy area around the hole). Look for dips, mounds and other contours. Try to visualise the route you want your ball to take from the moment you hit it until it goes into the hole.

THE RIGHT POSITION

Stand sideways-on to the hole. Your shoulders should be at right angles to the shaft of your club. Balance your weight equally on both feet to keep your body stable. You should be near enough to the ball to hit it without being cramped or leaning forwards. Always keep the blade at the bottom of your golf club flat.

THE RIGHT PUTTING MOTION

Grip the club in the palms of your hands, not with your fingers. Hold it firmly, but don't squeeze, as this will cause your shoulders to tense up which will affect the smoothness of your swing. You need to keep this steady grip throughout the putting action to make sure you keep your stroke smooth.

As you take your putt, your shoulders should move back as you raise the club and then forwards as you swing your arm to hit the ball. You should not flip or twist your hands when you putt.

THE GLOVE TRICK

If you need extra power for a long or uphill putt, it's very easy to lose control of your arms and shoulders – which spells disaster for your putt. To stop this happening, tuck a glove under the armpit of the arm that is closest to the hole. You should be able to keep the glove in place throughout the stroke.

AIM FOR A SMALL TARGET

Practising your putting action is essential. Stick two tees in the ground about 10 centimetres apart (tees are the small plastic stands that keep the ball from rolling around before you take a shot). Now aim to putt the ball between them. This is harder than sinking a ball into a hole, because any putts that are slightly off centre will just bounce off the tees. When you're out on the course, you'll find the holes seem much wider and you will be more likely to sink a ball.

HOW TO KEEP A PET SCORPION

Scorpions are popular pets and quite easy to look after. They usually live for up to six years. If you're interested in keeping scorpions, here are some tips to make sure you stay safe and your pet is always in peak condition.

CHOOSING THE RIGHT SCORPION

It's always a good idea to do your homework before you buy a pet. Visit a good pet shop for advice on which scorpion to own. The emperor scorpion is probably the most popular one to keep as a pet. This scorpion is black in colour, can grow up to about 20 centimetres in length and has a sting that is similar to that of a bee. Other scorpions that make good pets are Thai black scorpions and Javanese jungle scorpions.

Scorpions are not very sociable creatures, so it is fine to keep one on its own.

THE RIGHT HOUSING

Buy a glass tank with a lockable lid. A ten-gallon tank should be big enough for your new friend.

Scorpions like to be kept at a constant temperature of about 25°C. So to heat your tank, you will need a heatmat (this is an electrical device you can buy which sits just under the bottom of the tank). Make sure you turn the heatmat off if the temperature in your house rises above 25°C in hot weather.

You will need to give your scorpion a regular supply of water. Buy a shallow water container so your scorpion will not drown in it and add some stones at the bottom for your scorpion to walk on. Scorpions love to burrow and hide away, so add a log to the tank for it to crawl under.

It is important to ask the pet shop owner whether your scorpion is a species that originates from a rainforest area or a desert area. If your pet comes from a rainforest area, add a 6 centimetre layer of peat-free compost and cover it with orchid bark chipping. Keep the top layer damp with a daily spray of water. If your scorpion belongs to a desert species, you should add a deep layer (about 10 centimetres) of sand. (Ask at your local pet shop for advice on the best type of sand to use.)

THE RIGHT DIET

Scorpions are 'carnivores', which means they eat meat. You should feed them with crickets and mealworms that you can buy online or from a pet shop. Put food in for them two or three times a week. Always feed your pet at night, as this is when they would normally hunt and eat in the wild.

Warning. Never, ever handle your scorpion – they do sting and it is painful. Some scorpion stings can be extremely dangerous, so if you do get stung seek medical attention immediately. When feeding, cleaning or changing the water dish, always wait until your scorpion is away from the lid before you open the tank. Keep an eye on it all the time if the top is open and close the lid quickly if it moves towards the opening. Make sure the lid is locked when you have finished.

HOW TO MAKE A MISSISSIPPI MUD PIE

The Mississippi mud pie is a seriously chocolatey cake. Its name comes from its likeness to the muddy banks of the Mississippi river where the cake was invented. To make your own deliciously messy pie follow the simple recipe below.

You Will Need:

For The Crumb Base: • 100 g crushed digestive biscuits • 50 g butter, melted • 25 g demerara sugar
For The Filling: • 400 g dark chocolate • 225 g butter • two tablespoons boiling water • 300 ml single cream • 350 g dark muscovado sugar • six eggs • a 20 cm diameter loose-bottomed cake tin ... oh, and a squirt of whipped cream

WHAT YOU DO

1. Preheat the oven to 190°C/ 375°F/ Gas Mark 5. (Always get an adult to supervise when using an oven.) Grease your cake tin with a bit of butter.

2. To make the base, mix together the melted butter, crushed biscuits and demerara sugar. Spoon the mix into the bottom of your cake tin and flatten it down.

3. To make the filling, take a small saucepan filled with water to a depth of 5 centimetres, and place it on the hob and bring to the boil. Place a heatproof mixing bowl inside the saucepan. Break the chocolate into the bowl and stir in the butter and the two tablespoons of boiling water. Stir until completely melted.

4. Remove the bowl from the heat and beat in the single cream and muscovado sugar. Whisk in the eggs quickly to avoid scrambling them!

5. Pour the mixture into the tin, on top of the crumb base. Bake for an hour and fifteen minutes or until the top is slightly crunchy.

6. Allow to cool before carefully removing the cake from the tin. Serve with a big squirt of whipped cream. Mmmmm ...

HOW TO DRAW WITHOUT LIFTING YOUR PEN

Challenge a friend to draw the number 100 on a sheet of paper without lifting the pencil off the page between the separate figures. Impossible? No. Simply practise the steps shown below.

HOW TO RIDE BAREBACK

Ever imagined yourself riding bareback into the sunset like cowboys do in the movies? Before Hollywood comes knocking at your door you'll need to learn how.

PROFESSIONAL INSTRUCTION

It is essential to learn to ride bareback with an experienced rider or trained instructor, and to wear all the appropriate safety gear. However, here are some tips to remember.

- Choose a horse with a smooth riding action, a broad back and low 'withers' (the ridges between a horse's shoulder blades). All these factors make it easier for you to stay on the horse.

- Before attempting to ride bareback, practise riding with a saddle but without stirrups – this is a great way to prepare.

- Wear some extra padding in your trousers – bareback riding can be painful!

RIDING BAREBACK

1. Use a fixed platform to mount your horse. Once you're astride, take your time to get settled and balanced.

2. When you are ready, take the reins. Set off, making sure your instructor is walking beside you, leading the horse.

3. When you're under way, keep your head up and eyes focused on where you are heading. Don't look down, as this might make you sway on the horse's back.

4. Keep your legs long and relaxed, as if your body is sinking down through the horse's back. Resist the temptation to clench your thighs too much. Avoid digging your heels into the sides of your horse.

5. Keep your back straight. Try not to lean back, as this will push your legs too far forwards. If you lean forwards, your heels will also be in the wrong position.

6. If you feel you are slipping, don't grip your horse with your legs, this will only cause it to move faster. Ride em', cowboy!

HOW TO BREAKDANCE

Listen up. It's time to step up and pull some seriously slammin' shapes. Here's a move that requires plenty of practice and, more importantly, bags of confidence. Once you've mastered the steps below you can begin to improvise, creating your own personal breakdancing style.

1. Place your hands on the floor a little more than shoulder-width apart. Your legs should be spread a little wider.

2. Lift your right hand up and bring your left leg forward to the place where your right hand was.

3. Now bend your right leg behind your left leg, so that your right foot is almost directly under your bottom.

4. Next, you need to uncross your legs, keeping your right leg where it is and swinging your left leg out and under your bottom.

5. Shift your weight onto your right arm (the more of your weight that is on your hand, the faster your feet can move). Keeping your left leg where it is, swing your right leg in front and across your left leg, as shown.

6. Keeping your right hand where it is, step back with your left leg. This is the bit that will need some practice to perfect.

7. Now, simply put your right leg back into the starting position and put your left hand on the floor. Now repeat the six steps.

Top Tip. Don't try and do this move quickly until you can do the steps without having to think too hard. You should soon be able to make it look smooth and effortless.

Now show your crew what you can do!

HOW TO ABSEIL

Abseiling is a great way for climbers to descend a cliff face, mountain or even a building using ropes. It is used throughout the world during rescue operations, by people exploring caves, and in military activities. Here's some essential advice that will ensure you get to the bottom safely and in style.

Warning. Never attempt to abseil without being supervised. It is vital that you are shown how to abseil by a qualified instructor and that your equipment is professionally set up. You should wear all the necessary safety equipment, including helmet, safety harness and ropes.

THE WARM UP

Go for a run before you start. If your muscles are warmed up before you begin a descent, you will be able to stretch further and your legs will be able to hold you in place firmly at each level.

THE BASIC MOVE

Once your instructor has safely secured you in an abseiling harness, they will then attach a 'descender' device through a loop in the centre of your harness (a descender stops the rope from moving unless you feed it through with your hand, letting you descend a cliff at your own pace).

When you are ready to begin abseiling, stand at the top of the cliff with your back to the cliff edge. Gently lean back with your legs apart and step off the edge of the cliff. Your rope will keep you from falling. The take-off is the hardest part of abseiling so take your time. If you find it difficult, try sitting on the edge of the cliff and gently sliding off.

When both your feet are firmly against the face of the cliff, make a small jump away from the cliff face. As you jump, feed a short length of the rope through the descender by letting the rope slide through your hand. This will let through just enough rope for you to descend the cliff a small distance.

Make your own way down using this same technique, taking small gradual jumps until you reach the bottom.

SAFE DESCENT

- **Choose Your Next Spot Carefully.** At every stage, look down and find a suitable place to land. This should be relatively level and not obscured by any overhanging trees or loose rocks.

- **At Every Stage Make Sure You Are Stable.** Once you've reached your chosen landing spot, use your legs and feet to steady yourself.

- **Take It Slowly.** Abseiling down a cliff face does not in fact involve speed like it does in the movies. Jumping down too fast will put too much pressure on the rope and may also dislodge any loose rocks which could fall on you.

- **Don't Be Too Ambitious.** When abseiling, make small jumps. Small, controlled jumps are much more effective than long ones. They will give you more time to think about your next move and will ensure you don't make any silly mistakes that could cause you to slip.

ALSO AVAILABLE

The Boys' Book: How To
Be The Best At Everything
ISBN: 978-1-905158-64-5

The Boys' Book Of Survival:
How To Survive
Anything, Anywhere
ISBN: 978-1-906082-12-3

The Girls' Book: How To
Be The Best At Everything
ISBN: 978-1-905158-79-9

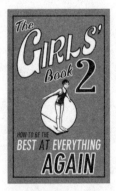

The Girls' Book 2:
How To Be The Best At
Everything Again
ISBN: 978-1-906082-32-1

The Girls' Book Of Glamour:
A Guide To Being A
Goddess
ISBN: 978-1-906082-13-0